BALLOONING

by Phyllis J. Perry

A FIRST BOOK

FRANKLIN WATTS
A DIVISION OF GROLIER PUBLISHING

NEW YORK   LONDON   HONG KONG   SYDNEY
DANBURY, CONNECTICUT

For Clare,
who loved her first
balloon ride!

Acknowledgments: Special thanks to L. Gale Abels and Robert J. Recks for helpful comments on this book and to E. Russell Primm III for his encouragement.

Photographs ©: AP/Wide World Photos: 30; Archive Photos: 28, 50–51; Bettmann Archive: 17 left; Brown Brothers: 17 right, 23; Comstock: cover, 2, 11, 34–35, 39, 40, 45, 52–53; Gamma-Liaison: 48 (Mark Greenberg/VISIONS); North Wind Picture Archives: 14; Peter W. Richardson: 9, 32, 55; PhotoEdit: 13 (Tom Prettyman); Stock Montage, Inc.: 19; Superstock, Inc.: 21; Tony Stone Images: 36; UPI/Bettmann: 26, 42.

Library of Congress Cataloging-in-Publication Data

Perry, Phyllis Jean.
    Ballooning / Phyllis J. Perry.
        p. cm. — (A First book)
    Includes bibliographical references and index.
    Summary: Describes the history of ballooning from its origins in eighteenth-century France to today.
    ISBN 0-531-20234-8 (lib. bdg.) ISBN 0-531-15807-1 (pbk.)
    1. Balloons—History—Juvenile literature. 2. Ballooning—History—Juvenile literature. [1. Hot air balloons. 2. Ballooning.] I. Title. II. Series.
TL616.P47 1996
629.133'22—dc20   96-7229 CIP AC

Contents

Chapter 1

Riding High in the Sky

Nothing is more colorful than balloons sailing high against a bright-blue sky. The brilliantly colored balloons hang like enormous ornaments in the air. Perhaps you have looked up and seen one of these balloons and wished that you might take a ride. If you went for a ride, your adventure might go something like this:

You wake up early in the morning and check the weather. There is no sign of a thunderstorm, and there are none forecast for the next thirty-six hours. The air is cool and a gentle breeze of 2 to 6 miles (3 to 10 km) per

You need an open field to lay out the balloon envelope.

hour is blowing. It is a perfect day for a hot-air balloon ride.

First you meet the ground crew at the takeoff site, a grassy surface with a long, unobstructed distance downwind. The crew spreads out the huge balloon **envelope** across the field. You lay the basket on its side and hook it to the envelope using about twenty color-coded cables.

After the pilot has checked the fuel system for leaks, you hold open the **mouth** of the balloon. At the same time, a ground crew member starts a large engine-driven fan, which rests on the ground between the basket and the envelope. The cool air blows into the balloon and inflates the envelope.

As the balloon begins to fill with cool air, you help the ground crew check for rips or tears in the envelope. Everything appears to be in good shape.

While some members of the crew wearing protective gloves hold open the mouth of the balloon, the pilot opens the blast valve of the **gas burner**. Quick blasts of flame shoot into the balloon, accompanied by loud roaring noises. You feel your heart beating fast. You're a little nervous to take your first flight!

With each blast of flame, the air inside the balloon gets warmer. You and the rest of the ground crew hold on to the basket tightly so it does not rise too soon. Finally, you turn the basket upright and climb in to keep it steady while the pilot completes preparations for ascent.

On a signal from the pilot, the members of the ground crew release the basket. The pilot turns the burner on again and gives several blasts. The balloon gently lifts off from the ground. The wind pushes it up and across the grassy field until the balloon is skimming over the trees and rising higher and higher.

Holding open the mouth of the balloon and operating
the gas burner requires several hands.

From this perch you can see treetops, fields, and the enormous shadow of your balloon. The balloon travels with the wind. Onboard is a compass and flight instruments to help your pilot know in which direction you are traveling and how high in the air you are.

Once you are sailing, the burner is normally operated for five seconds and then turned off for about twenty seconds, and so on. More frequent burning causes the balloon to rise; less burning makes it descend.

When the burner is off, you notice how beautifully quiet it is up in the sky. Floating in the air, you have a completely different view of the world. When it is time for your glorious first balloon flight to end, the pilot uses the blast valve less, and you wait for the air inside the balloon to cool.

Slowly, the balloon begins to sink until it is flying just above the trees. You spy a good, open field ahead. The balloon pilot checks by radio with the ground crew. The crew gets permission from the farmer to land in his field and radios this information back to the pilot.

With permission to land, the pilot releases the vent. The hot air escapes and the basket lands in the field with a thump. Quickly, the balloon pilot tugs a cord. The top of the bal-

loon opens and the hot air rushes out.

The ground crew comes to help pack up. You stuff the long balloon into a cloth bag and load the bag, basket, and burners into a van. You have now joined the many people throughout history and the world who dreamed of and succeeded in floating through the sky. As you drive away, you are probably already planning your next ballooning adventure.

Riding high in the sky in a hot-air balloon is an extraordinary experience.

**The Montgolfiers launched one of
the first hot-air balloons in 1783.**

Chapter 2

Ballooning's Beginnings

During the late 1700s, two French papermakers, brothers Joseph and Etienne Montgolfier, were experimenting with parachutes and balloons. After many unsuccessful designs and schemes, the Montgolfier brothers carried out an interesting experiment with a large paper-and-cloth bag. They held the bag over a smoking fire and allowed the bag to fill with heated air. When they released the bag, it rose to the ceiling. This simple experiment was the beginning of ballooning.

After moving their balloon experiments outdoors, on June 5, 1783, the Montgolfiers sent up a balloon in the crowded village square of Annonay, France, amazing the villagers. They called it an aerostatic machine, or **aerostat**. Over the next several months, the Montgolfiers continued to work on their balloons, which became known as montgolfiers.

After noticing that the aerostat came down when the air cooled off, they explored ways for the aerostat to carry heat with it. But attaching a metal container to hold fire made the aerostat too heavy. So the Montgolfiers made another aerostat that was much bigger and would hold far more hot air. This new aerostat, the *Marianne*, went up 1,000 feet (305 m) and carried 40 pounds (18 kg).

Then, Joseph and Etienne Montgolfier built an even larger aerostat, the *Ad Astra*. The *Ad Astra* was 35 feet (11 m) in diameter. It was so big that it had to be constructed in four sections, which were buttoned together.

As news got out about the Montgolfier brothers' flying machines, many other scientists in France began experimenting with their own aerostats. People throughout the country started to clamor for a public exhibition, and the Montgolfiers were invited to show their aerostat to the king of France.

Because Joseph Montgolfier did not like public functions, Etienne and some friends, including Jean-

Joseph and Etienne Montgolfier

François Pilâtre de Rozier, took on the task of preparing an aerostat. Etienne and his crew built an impressive, oval-shaped aerostat called the *Revellion*. The balloon was covered in paper decorated with images of the king of France and his monogram. Unfortunately, a storm destroyed the *Revellion* before the king could see it.

Not wanting to disappoint the king, Etienne Montgolfier's crew worked night and day for a week to build another aerostat—the *Revellion II*. When the *Revellion II* ascended over Paris on September 19, 1783, it carried three animals from the royal barnyard as test passengers: a duck, a sheep, and a rooster.

After a short time in the air, the *Revellion II* came down in a forest about 2 miles (3 km) away. During the landing, the lid of the animals' basket broke open. When they were found, the birds stood outside the basket and the sheep was nibbling grass.

The *Revellion III* was built to carry a man and was to be demonstrated before the king at Versailles. Early hot-air balloons were powered by anything that would burn and produce lots of smoke, including damp straw or rags soaked in brandy. To make the *Revellion III* less likely to catch fire, both the inside and outside of the aerostat were coated with a metal called alum. The king, however, refused to allow human passengers in the Montgolfiers' balloon, with one exception. He agreed to allow a prisoner—who would receive a pardon if he survived the flight—to volunteer to go up, but that plan was never carried out.

What the king did at last agree to was to let a man go up in a balloon that was tethered. On October 15, 1783, Jean-François Pilâtre de Rozier became the first human passenger to ride in a tethered hot-air balloon. With long ropes attached to it, the *Revellion III* went up 80 feet (24 m).

A little more than a month later, the king was finally persuaded to allow men to go up in an untethered balloon. Pilâtre de Rozier and the marquis François Laurent d'Arlandes made the first manned free flight on November 21, 1783. The two men went

Jean-François Pilâtre de Rozier plunged to his death when his hydrogen balloon caught fire.

up 3,000 feet (914 m) in the air, traveled over 5 miles (8 km), and flew for 25 minutes.

In the history of ballooning, Pilâtre de Rozier is unfortunately remembered for another first. In 1785, Pilâtre de Rozier and his assistant went up in a **gondola** attached to double balloons, one inside the other. The outside balloon was filled with a gas lighter than air called hydrogen, and the inside balloon was filled with hot air. When the hydrogen balloon caught fire, Pilâtre de Rozier was killed in the world's first balloon tragedy.

At the same time that the Montgolfiers were working on hot-air balloons, Jacques Alexandre Charles, a French chemist, was experimenting with hydrogen-filled balloons. He sent up his first balloon on August 27, 1783. The unmanned aerostat climbed to an altitude of approximately 3,000 feet (914 m) and flew a distance of 15 miles (24 km).

That same year, Charles and an assistant made their first manned flight in a hydrogen-filled balloon. They reached a height of 2,000 feet (610 m) and were carried 25 miles (40 km) by the wind. On a later solo flight, Charles was able to take a balloon to a height of 9,000 feet (2,745 m).

After France's pioneering aerostat voyages, others around the world began ballooning. In 1784, Vincent Lunardi, an Italian living in London, made England's first manned balloon flight and Edward Warren became the first person to go up in a tethered hot-air balloon in the United States (over Baltimore, Maryland). That same year, too, Elisabeth Thible of France became the first female **aeronaut**.

Another French balloonist, Jean Pierre Blanchard, set plenty of records early on. Blanchard, traveling with an American doctor, John Jeffries, made the first aerial crossing of the English Channel in 1785. On January 9, 1793, at Philadelphia, Blanchard made the first U.S. manned balloon ascent. The audience

The first aerial crossing of the English Channel took place in 1785.

that witnessed the historic flight included President George Washington.

Experimenting with balloons continued into the 1800s. In 1839, the American balloonist John Wise invented the **rip panel**, a pull-away section at the top of the balloon used to release air or gas quickly on landing. Wise next undertook to sail across the Atlantic Ocean. Before attempting the trip, he tested his balloon, the *Atlantic*, on a flight that took off from St. Louis, Missouri, in 1859. Blown by a storm, the *Atlantic* set a distance record of 809 miles (1,302 km) in 19 hours and 50 minutes before crashing to the ground. Wise never succeeded in his efforts to cross the Atlantic Ocean in a balloon and he eventually abandoned the project.

In 1860, Samuel Archer King made a notable balloon flight over Boston, Massachusetts. He carried with him James Wilson Black, who took the first aerial photos of the United States. King also carried the first "balloon" mail, complete with a balloon postage stamp.

In 1861, the Civil War interrupted exhibiting and experimenting with ballooning in America. A few balloons, however, were used during the Civil War by both the North and South to watch troop positions. After the war, there was a revival of civilian ballooning.

In this Civil War photograph, soldiers inflate gas balloons to send up for information gathering.

Chapter 3

Investigating with Balloons

During World War I, hydrogen-filled gas balloons were used for observation. These huge balloons were fastened by reels of long, strong cables to trucks on the ground. As the cables were reeled out or in, the balloons soared up in the air or were hauled back down again. Hanging in baskets from these observation balloons, soldiers were able to observe troop positions and direct artillery fire.

After World War I, the U.S. Army shifted its use of balloons to nonmilitary activities. It formed an alliance with the National Geographic Society to use balloons to study the upper atmosphere. In 1927, scientific aeronaut Captain Hawthorne C. Gray rose in a balloon to 42,470 feet (12,945 m), more than 8 miles (13 km), above the earth.

Equipped with an oxygen mask, Gray kept a diary in the sky, taking notes of the temperature at different elevations. Gray learned that at 31,000 feet (9,450 m) the temperature was −32°F (−36°C). He made his last diary entry at 44,000 feet (13,410 m). When his balloon was recovered near Sparta, Tennessee, two days later, Captain Gray was found dead. Gray's diary is on display today in the Smithsonian Institution in Washington, D.C.

Another famous balloon experimenter was Auguste Piccard, a Swiss physicist who was eager to study cosmic rays. Piccard designed a round aluminum cabin that attached to an enormous balloon. In the spring of 1931, Piccard and his assistant took off from Augsburg, Germany, and rose 51,775 feet (15,780 m) above the earth. In his second attempt a year later, Piccard went even higher—53,149 feet (16,200 m). Auguste Piccard's twin brother, Jean Piccard, made his first cosmic ray studies aloft in 1934.

Just before World War II began, another famous balloon, the *Explorer II,* was launched. Captains Albert W. Stevens and Orvil A. Anderson went up

Albert W. Stevens (center) and Orvil A. Anderson
(left) stand with the alternate pilot in front
of the *Explorer II*'s gondola.

in a round metal gondola from a South Dakota launch site. On November 11, 1935, dressed in warm clothes and outfitted with enough oxygen to keep them alive, Stevens and Anderson reached a height of 72,395 feet (22,066 m). On the flight, the two men carried scientific instruments to gather information about high altitude. Although flies that they brought with them died, the eggs laid during the flight hatched. They also learned from air samples that bacteria could be carried from the ground through the air to miles above the earth.

In the early 1950s, monkeys and mice were sent up with various instruments to learn more about the effects of cosmic rays. Four monkeys that became famous for their flight were named Eenie, Meenie, Miney, and Moe. They went up to 121,000 feet (36,880 m), stayed aloft for 29 hours, and returned to earth safely.

About the same time, Navy scientists Malcolm D. Ross and M. Lee Lewis went up in several balloons made of a new, strong, lightweight material called plastic. On one of these launches, Charles Moore, a meteorologist, went along to study weather and sent the first televised pictures back to earth on October 18, 1957, from a height of 40,000 feet (12,190 m). Two years later, they repeated the feat from a height of 85,000 feet (25,910 m).

The scientific data collected by balloons over
the years has contributed greatly to the study
of the earth's atmosphere.

With each attempt to go higher in a balloon, scientists learned more about the many layers of air above the earth. The first layer above the earth, the troposphere, is about 7 miles (11 km) thick. The next layer, which reaches 60 miles (97 km) above the earth, is the stratosphere. The third layer is the ionosphere, the top side of which is 200 miles (322 km) above the earth. Next is the exosphere, or what we call outer space, which goes on for billions of miles into the universe.

In 1959, a group of scientists studying the planet Venus turned to balloonists to collect the data they needed. In an effort to discover whether water vapor exists on Venus, they built a telescope and sent it up in a balloon manned by Malcolm D. Ross and Charles Moore. The two balloonists took the telescope up more than 80,000 feet (24,385 m) in their helium-filled balloon. When light from Venus came through the telescope, it struck an electronic cell, which triggered another mechanism that drew a graph. Back on the ground, scientists studied these line drawings and determined that there is indeed water vapor on Venus.

With manned space flight came less interest in high-altitude, manned balloon flights. Two of the last major balloon flights occurred in the 1960s. In May 1961, Malcolm D. Ross and Victor Prather tested space

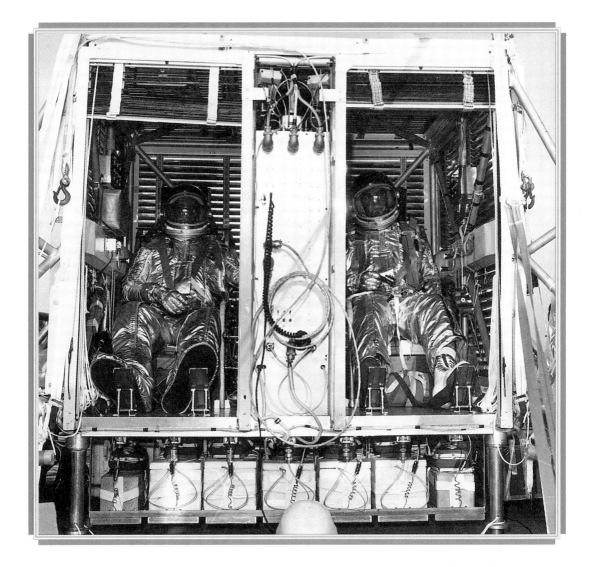

In 1961, two Navy scientists, Victor Prather
(left) and Malcolm D. Ross, made the
highest manned balloon ascent.

suits developed for the *Mercury* astronauts. They went up to 113,740 feet (34,668 m) and landed in the Gulf of Mexico. On February 1, 1966, aeronaut Nick Piantanida made a balloon flight to 123,800 feet (37,734 m) with a descent by parachute. On his next flight, he was killed while attempting to go even higher.

Balloons come in all shapes and sizes.

Chapter 4

Balloooning for Fun

Ballooning appeals to ordinary people as well as to those who are out to set world records or conduct research. With the technological and safety improvements in both hot-air and gas balloons has come renewed interest in ballooning as a sport.

Ballooning enthusiasts and pilots have been members of the Balloon Federation of America since 1961. Today, there are several thousand certified balloon pilots in the United States.

Balloon pilot training schools are open to young people as well to adults. Students can begin training at age fourteen and are eligible for licensing at sixteen. To earn a private pilot license, a student pilot needs at least ten hours of flying time, ground training, and a passing score on a written test that covers the basics of ballooning. Students must also pass a test flight accompanied by a pilot examiner approved by the Federal Aviation Administration (FAA). In addition, the FAA inspects all balloons, which are legally classified as aircraft, before they can fly.

Before getting licensed, the students learn about flight rules and regulations, wind and weather, and flight plans. They also learn about balloon construction, as well as how to assemble, inflate, and anchor a balloon.

Today's hot-air balloons have several parts: the burner assembly, the envelope, the suspension system, and the basket. A complete set of technical instruments is also crucial for safe flying.

Learning how to inflate the huge envelope of a balloon is an important part of becoming a pilot

Balloon pilots rely on the gas burner to control the hot-air balloon in the sky.

The burner assembly uses propane to heat the air. The heater is located at the mouth of the balloon. As the air is heated, it expands and becomes lighter than the surrounding air. The hot air, trapped inside the envelope, pushes upward and lifts the basket off the ground.

The burners are connected by hoses to one or two tanks of liquid propane, which are secured in the basket. A 20-gallon (76-l) tank of propane will keep a balloon up for about three hours. The pilot uses a blast valve to squirt propane into the burners. When the air in the envelope cools and the balloon begins to descend, the pilot uses the burner again to control the balloon's altitude.

Balloon envelopes come in many designs and some fantastic shapes. Many of these colorful bags are made of rip-stop nylon, usually coated with a sealant to resist abrasion and sun damage. Envelopes are made by sewing together long panels, or gores, of fabric.

Balloon envelopes have an inflation **skirt** attached to the bottom. The skirt is made from fireproof fabric. It directs heat up into the balloon and also prevents the envelope from being scorched by flames from the burner.

A balloon envelope might remind you a little of a giant parachute. A typical balloon envelope weighs 120 pounds (54 kg). Although it looks huge, the envelope can be packed into a 3-foot (almost 1-m) canvas bag when deflated.

Envelopes vary in size depending upon their purpose. Small balloons, like the AX-1, are ultralight. An AX-5 envelope is big enough to carry one person comfortably. Balloons classified as AX-6 to AX-9 can carry up to eight people.

To descend, pilots open vents in the envelope. In the side of the envelope of older balloons is a small, self-closing slot called the **maneuvering vent**, which can be opened by pulling a cord that hangs into the basket. The pilot opens the vent, allowing hot air to escape and causing the balloon to drop. Most balloons, however, now use the **parachute vent**, which is a small parachute plugging a hole in the envelope.

On landing, the pilot pulls a red nylon cord that hangs from the rip panel. When the Velcro-held rip panel opens at the top of the envelope, the hot air rushes out and the balloon deflates entirely.

The suspension system includes flat, webbed nylon ropes called load tapes. These tapes are stitched over the vertical seams that join the envelope panels and meet at the top of the balloon. The lower ends of the tapes are connected to stainless-steel wires, or suspension cables, and support the burner assembly and the basket.

The basket, or gondola, carries the balloon load, which includes the burner assembly, fuel, and the

Stainless-steel suspension cables, which attach to ropes that extend over the top of the balloon, support the burner assembly and the basket.

Flight instruments measure the balloon's
temperature, speed, and altitude.

passengers. Gondolas are made of aluminum tubing or wicker. A typical basket to hold four people is about waist high and measures 3 feet by 4 feet (90 cm by 122 cm). The rim of the basket is often padded with foam and covered in buckskin. Although aluminum-tubing gondolas have the advantage of being lightest, wicker baskets have more "give" to cushion the shock of a hard landing.

Balloonists also carry flight instruments, including a compass, a **pyrometer** to measure the air temperature near the top of the envelope, an **altimeter** to measure the height above the ground, and a **variometer** to measure the rate of rise or descent of the balloon. They also carry navigation charts, a radio for communication with the ground crew, an envelope temperature gauge, a burner pressure gauge, and fuel gauges.

A variety of weather factors from wind speed to air temperature affect both the safety and duration of balloon flights. For example, because air is colder in the winter, the air inside the envelope does not have to be heated as much to make it lighter than the outside air. For this reason, the propane fuel (and the flights) last longer in the winter than in the summer.

Gas balloons are quite different from hot-air balloons. First, they are considerably more expensive to fly. In 1995, a hot-air inflation for two aeronauts

Unlike hot-air balloons, gas balloons have a tube at the bottom of the envelope called an appendix and carry weights called ballasts.

was estimated at $150 while a similar helium balloon inflation cost $2,000. Ammonia, which is used for most gas flights in the United States today, costs about $50. Second, it takes a crew of about ten people to launch a gas balloon while half that number can easily launch a hot-air balloon.

The earliest gas balloons used hydrogen, which proved dangerous because this gas is flammable when mixed with air. Many people, however, continue to make thousands of safe flights a year using hydrogen.

A tube called the **appendix** is used to inflate a gas balloon. The appendix remains open during flight to allow excess gas to escape and keep the envelope from bursting.

To cause a gas balloon to rise, weights called **ballasts** are dropped from the balloon. Ballasts are usually bags of sand, but they can be anything heavy. As a gas balloon rises, the air pressure around it decreases, and the gas inside the balloon expands.

To descend, the balloonist lets some of the gas out of the envelope through a valve at the top of the balloon. This is called valving. Landing a gas balloon is much like landing a hot-air balloon. The balloonist in a gas balloon opens a rip panel to deflate the balloon quickly. This prevents dragging the basket and its passengers along the ground if the wind is blowing.

People who are about to take up any balloon— hot-air or gas—must be be mindful of current and future weather conditions. Unexpected thunderstorms, high winds, and wind shears (sudden changes in wind speed and direction over a short distance) can be extremely dangerous for balloons in flight.

Balloonists must also be careful of thermals. A thermal is a column of hot air formed when the sun warms the ground. If a balloon runs into this current of warm air, it may rise at a rapid rate. The center of a thermal has swirling air that may swing the basket wildly. Also, if a balloon is in a thermal, and then moves out of it, the balloon will suddenly lose lift. It is preferable to balloon in the early morning to avoid thermals, which occur mostly in the late afternoon.

Although experienced balloon pilots and improved technology have made ballooning safer than ever, accidents can always happen. High-wind landings cause baskets to flip; fires flare up while fueling; tether lines break; wind blows envelopes into power lines. Balloons can even cause accidents on the ground: balloons floating past in the sky have been known to startle horses, causing them to bolt and throw riders.

The fundamental rules of flying safe are: don't fly when the weather is bad, maintain safe altitudes, and be especially careful when refueling.

Good balloonists always pay attention
to changing weather conditions.

Chapter 5

Current Ballooning Challenges

One of the most exciting events of modern-day ballooning history was the first flight across the Atlantic Ocean. Three Americans, Ben Abruzzo, Maxie Anderson, and Larry Newman, completed the voyage in their helium balloon, the *Double Eagle II*, in 1978.

More recently, in February 1995, American balloonist Steve Fossett became the first person to fly a balloon solo across the Pacific Ocean. He set a world distance record of 5,432 miles (8,742 km) in 4 days, 6 hours, and 15 minutes. Fossett, a millionaire stockbroker, left Seoul, South Korea, and landed in a farmer's field near Leader, in the Canadian province of Saskatchewan. In January 1996, Fossett tried unsuccessfully to circle the world in a nonstop flight in his yellow *Solo Challenger* capsule.

Many regard circling the globe in a balloon to be the greatest unachieved goal in aviation. Since the mid-1990s, at least five balloon teams have been vying to be the first to ride the winds all the way around the world in a balloon. Team members are an international group. It is probably only a matter of time before someone at last succeeds.

The *Earthwinds* balloon team has been working to fly a 360-foot (110-m) double balloon around the world since 1995. They plan to use a huge polyethylene helium balloon and a smaller compressed-air ballast balloon. The *Earthwinds* contains a closed capsule to supply oxygen, electric power, and living quarters for a three-person crew. The balloon carries two liquid helium containers to replace helium gas in flight and a 450-gallon (1,703-l) gasoline tank to power the onboard engines. The crew hopes to fly west to east with a flying time of nine to thirteen days at an approximate altitude of 35,000 feet (10,670 m).

The *Holland-Flyer* balloon crew, using a balloon with compound helium and hot air, also plans to fly west to east. They estimate eight to twelve days for

The *Earthwinds* team plans to use two balloons on its sail around the world: one helium balloon (top) and one compressed-air balloon (bottom).

the round-the-world journey at an approximate altitude of 35,000 feet (10,670 m). This crew is using two generators for its power supply.

The *Odyssey* crew, using a simple helium balloon with batteries and solar panels for a power supply, plans to fly east to west. They estimate a flight of eighteen to twenty-two days at an altitude of 120,000 feet (36,575 m) by day and 75,000 feet (22,860 m) by night.

The *Windstar* crew, using a balloon type known as a cocoon, which consists of a helium lift and compressed-air ballast, relies on two generators for its power supply. The crew plans to fly west to east at an altitude of 35,000 feet (10,670 m). The estimated flight time is eight to twelve days.

The *Endeavor* plans to fly a balloon using the combined lifting power of helium and hot air and to launch from Australia. However, this group has not received the financial backing necessary to finish development and flight plans. Such attempts require millions of dollars.

Other ballooning challenges include regional and international rallies, which bring together balloonists from all over the world. These events test many ballooning skills. In hare-and-hounds races, the "hare" balloon takes off first and "hound" balloons try to land as close to the hare balloon as possible. In the "elbow bender" event, pilots work to achieve

International rallies provide balloonists
with some spectacular views.

the greatest degree of bend in the course of their flight. In "jack-in-the-box" events, pilots try to be the first to inflate their balloon and fly over the finish line.

Ballooning contests began in 1906 with the Gordon Bennett balloon race. This distance contest for gas balloons continues to be held at various sites throughout the world.

Since then, many different rallies have been established in the United States and abroad. The U.S. National Hot-Air Balloon Championships have been held each summer since 1963 in various cities across the country. The first Balloon Fiesta was held in Albuquerque, New Mexico, in 1972. Every October since then, Albuquerque hosts the International Balloon Fiesta, which is the world's largest rally.

Another international rally is the World Hot-Air Balloon Championships. The twelfth of these championships took place in July 1995 in Battle Creek, Michigan, and the United States swept all three

In competition, the skies fill with colorful balloons.

medals. The 1997 World Hot-Air Ballooning Championships will be held in Saga, Japan.

International ballooning competition took a major stride in 1995. For the first time since World War II, Eastern Bloc countries opened their airspace to balloon flight; balloonists all over the world celebrated.

Only months after the announcement, a ballooning tragedy occurred. During the Thirty-Ninth Coupe Gordon Bennett Gas Balloon Distance Race, a balloon carrying the U.S. Virgin Islands flag and all required permissions for the flight was shot from the sky by a Belarussian military helicopter. The two American balloonists on board were killed. Although the ballooning world was shaken and greatly saddened by the incident, after an investigation, officials decided against banning future ballooning events over Belarus.

Ballooning continues to be an exciting sport. Every year new records are broken. Perhaps one day, you, or your friend, or a relative, will be on the ground crew or among those who race in the skies across Europe, North America, New Zealand, or elsewhere in the world. Perhaps you will be the historic balloonist who breaks the final frontier and becomes the first to fly in a balloon around the globe.

It is important to remember that the joy of modern ballooning, our probes into space, and the ease of modern airplane flight would not have been

Some young balloonists have caught ballooning fever.

possible without the information first acquired by early aeronauts. Their experiments, mere whispers in the air, formed the foundation of modern flight and space exploration.

Ballooning Terms

aeronaut — an operator of a balloon or airship

aerostat — any lighter-than-air aircraft

altimeter — an instrument used to measure altitude

appendix — the tube at the bottom of a gas balloon used to inflate the envelope

ballast — the weight carried by operators of gas balloons to control altitude

envelope — the huge cotton, plastic, or nylon bag that holds the air or gas in a balloon

gas burner — the unit carried between the skirt and gondola to burn propane gas and heat the air that fills the envelope of a hot-air balloon

gondola — the basket or enclosed cabin for passengers and equipment that a balloon carries

maneuvering vent — the slot in a hot-air balloon's envelope that the pilot pulls open with a cord to release air in small amounts and thereby control altitude

mouth — the large opening at the bottom of a balloon's envelope

parachute vent — the small parachute plugging a hole in a hot-air balloon's envelope that the pilot opens to descend quickly

pyrometer — an instrument used to measure high temperatures

rip panel — the section of an envelope that the pilot pulls open with a cord to release the air quickly for landing

skirt — the heat-resistant-fabric extension of the envelope designed to channel the heated air safely into the mouth of a hot-air balloon

variometer — a vertical-speed indicator that measures the rate of climb or descent

Organizations
and Publications

ORGANIZATIONS

The Balloon Federation of America
P.O. Box 400
Indianola, IA 50125

National Balloon Museum
P.O. Box 149
Indianola, IA 50125

BOOKS

Belville, Cheryl W. *Flying in a Hot Air Balloon.* Minneapolis: Carolrhoda, 1993.

Coombs, Charles. *Hot-air Ballooning.* New York: William Morrow, 1981.

Kaner, Etta. *Balloon Science.* Reading, Mass.: Addison-Wesley, 1990.

Newman, Ed. *Hot Air and Gas: The Basics of Balloons.* Roseland, Va.: Greenway, 1992.

Paulsen, Gary. *Full of Hot Air: Launching, Floating High, and Landing.* New York: Delacorte, 1993.

Waligunda, Bob, and Larry Sheehan. *Great American Balloon Book: An Introduction to Hot-Air Ballooning.* Englewood Cliffs, N.J.: Prentice-Hall, 1981.

Wirth, Dick, and Jerry Young. *Ballooning: The Complete Guide to Riding the Winds.* New York: Random House, 1984.

MAGAZINES

Ballooning
P.O. Box 400
Indianola, IA 50125

Balloon Life
2145 Dale Avenue
Sacramento, CA 95815

Resources on the Internet

For information about recreational ballooning, check out *Balloon Life* magazine's World Wide Web page at the following address:

> **http://www.aero.com/publications/
> balloon_life/bl.htm**

For scientific information about ballooning, check out NASA's scientific ballooning program World Wide Web page at the following address:

> **http://lheawww.gsfc.nasa.gov/docs/
> balloon/balloon_top.html**

For information about the *Odyssey* expedition, check out its World Wide Web page at the following address:

> **http://www.viva.com/odyssey**

Index

About the Author

Phyllis J. Perry has written two dozen books for teachers and young people, including *The Fiddle-hoppers: Crickets, Katydids, and Locusts* and *Sea Stars and Dragons* for Franklin Watts. She received her doctorate in curriculum and instruction from the University of Colorado, where she currently supervises student teachers. Dr. Perry lives with her husband, David, in Boulder, Colorado.